# SAMSON

## LIFE LESSONS FROM A FLAWED HERO

# AL GLUCHOSKI

# SAMSON

## – LIFE LESSONS FROM A FLAWED HERO

ISBN: 0-9755311-1-5

Published by

LIFEBRIDGE
B O O K S
P.O. BOX 49428
CHARLOTTE, NC 28277

Printed in the United States of America.

## DEDICATION

*I dedicate this book to my beautiful wife, Lorraine, and to my wonderful daughters, Tiffany and Victoria. Their support, help and understanding has allowed me to pursue God's call on my life. I would be incomplete without them.*

*Special thanks to Dennis and Vikki Burke for their help and encouragement with this project, to Marianne Mongrello for her valuable assistance and to my partners for their continual support.*

# CONTENTS

# INTRODUCTION

Together, we are about to take a marvelous journey back in time—examining the life of the heroic strongman of scripture, Samson. We will discover how character and integrity, or a lack thereof, can effect our life's outcome and destiny.

With great power and anointing comes the responsibility of properly caring for such a gifting. In short, conduct does matter!

Strong values and moral principles must be at the foundation of every endeavor we undertake. Without these, a great anointing cannot be sustained.

In Samson's life, a failure to demonstrate godly character led him to experience the classic "bad hair day" in all of history! Certainly, he had memorable moments of faith and victory, yet he also committed glaring errors of disobedience. Unfortunately, when it was all said and done, his poor stewardship of God's gifting in his life caused his days to end prematurely, only partially completing his assignment.

On these pages we will look at Samson's successes and downfalls, and discover how they serve as an example to us today.

Our headlines are filled with scandals of all shades being uncovered for public viewing—corporate scandals, political lies, cheating in professional athletics and sexual misconduct of leaders. It seems each week there is a new revelation, both in the "world" and, sadly, in the church.

Now, more than ever, it's time for character and integrity to be exhibited clearly through God's people.

May the Lord speak to your heart and strengthen your life as you take this revealing journey with me.

*— Al Gluchoski*

*Being a parent is not a job for cowards or compromisers. It is a sacred responsibility.*

– Al Gluchoski

# 1

# The Birth of a Deliverer

As a young boy, even before my days as a football player, I loved to read about Hercules—the mythical Greek hero who could defeat whole armies by himself. Enthralled, I read how he killed a lion with his bare hands and destroyed a large temple by pushing down its pillars!

I remember wanting to be just like him, but after all, Hercules was only a myth. To my amazement, I discovered in the pages of scripture that a real "Hercules" had actually existed. His name was Samson.

Later on my spiritual journey, after digging deep into God's Word, I began to realize the importance of this Biblical character, and the vital life lessons you and I can learn from the story of this flawed hero.

## Who Would Free the People?

Let me take you back to the time of the Judges, several hundred years after the Exodus, when Israel had no king. "God's chosen people" were living under the rule of the Philistines—where we get the name Palestine today.

Their circumstances were the direct result of blatant sin and disobedience. The Bible declares: *"The children of Israel did evil again in the sight of the Lord; and the Lord delivered them into the hand of the Philistines"* (Judges 13:1).

**INIQUITY ALWAYS LEADS TO BONDAGE OR SOME FORM OF CAPTIVITY.**

Even in these early times, God made it clear that iniquity always leads to bondage or some form of captivity.

Obviously, they didn't understand the secret of living righteous before the Lord—to simply, "stop sinning!"

To make matters worse, the Israelites had become rather apathetic and, with little question, accepted the rule of the Philistines as their lot in life.

God, however, desired that someone should rise up and make war against the enemy, not simply to co-exist with them on the land. This was the passion of the Almighty for His people—to bring a deliverer who would free Israel from the dominance of ungodly rulers.

## Out of Weakness

The Philistines were an intimidating bunch, artfully skilled in psychological warfare. Even their armor and battle dress was designed to strike fear in the hearts of their enemies. This is what they had done with Israel— especially to the tribe of Dan, who surrendered their land to the advancing Philistines and retreated to the north.

**A MAN WAS ABOUT TO BE BORN WHO WOULD SET ISRAEL IN A NEW DIRECTION.**

As we will see, however, out of this tribe of the *intimidated,* God would raise up the *intimidator.* Out of the weak would come the strong! A man was about to be born who would set Israel in a new direction—on a path toward eventual freedom.

## The Nazarite

An angel of the Lord appeared to a barren woman, the wife of Manoah. He tells her she is going to give birth to a son who will *"begin to deliver Israel out of the hand of the Philistines"* (Judges 13:5).

Specifically, God instructed that this child *"shall be a Nazarite to God from the womb to the day of his death"* (v.7).

The Nazarite vow, described in Numbers 6:1-6, calls for total separation and holiness unto the Lord. It includes these four directives:

1. You shall not eat any grapes or product of the vine.
2. You cannot touch any dead body—animal or human.
3. You shall not drink any wine or strong drink.
4. No razor must come to your head.

Any violation of these rules would be considered sin, accompanied by God's chastening!

**THE SON WHO WAS ABOUT TO BE BORN TO THIS BARREN WOMAN WAS TO BE A LIFELONG NAZARITE WHO WOULD FULFILL GOD'S PURPOSES AND CALLING.**

If a Nazarite *did* touch a corpse, he was to shave his head, go through cleansing, and then be given a fresh start as a Nazarite once again.

Normally, one would take this vow for a certain period of time by his own choice, but the son who was to be born to this barren woman was to be a *lifelong* Nazarite who would fulfill God's purposes and calling.

## "How Shall We Raise Him?"

The woman told her husband, Manoah, of her

experience, and he cried out for God to send the angel again—to tell them how to raise this special child. God answered his prayer and sent the angel once more to his wife, but Manoah was not with her!

Immediately, she runs to get her husband and he asks the angel, "Are you the one who spoke to my wife?" And the angel replies, "I am."

Manoah continues, "Please, tell us how to raise this child."

The angel responds by repeating everything the woman was to observe. Manoah's personal question went unanswered. No real specifics were directed to him.

## An Awesome Encounter

I believe the angel's "silence" toward the question was actually deafening! In other words, the angel was admonishing Manoah, "I've already given instructions from God to your wife; raise this child as a Nazarite. Teach him with God's Word. Love and nurture him and when necessary, correct and discipline him. He is called to be a deliverer, but he will need guidance and proper training."

In many cases, you don't receive further instructions from God until the first set of orders have been obeyed.

The couple then offered a sacrifice to God and the angel departed towards heaven. The encounter was so awesome, Manoah exclaimed to his wife, *"We shall surely die, because we have seen God"* (Judges 13:22).

Her response, however, is very telling. She basically says, "If God kills us, how are we going to have the son  He has promised?"

> "IF GOD KILLS US, HOW ARE WE GOING TO HAVE THE SON HE HAS PROMISED?"

It becomes apparent that the wife is more "in tune with the Lord" than Manoah!  The Amplified Bible even calls the woman more "sensible" than her husband. This may explain why the angel appeared to *her* and not *him!*

## The Father's Role

In my opinion, this reveals a problem. Manoah does not seem to be the "spiritual leader" in this home, which opens the door to disorder in the household.

As is common today, Manoah may have been more preoccupied with being the *bread winner* and *provider* than he was in being the "prayer warrior" of his home.

The Bible is emphatic that the man is to lead and guide his family spiritually under the leadership of the Holy Spirit!  This was true in that early culture and remains God's will for today.

Scripture records: *"...the woman bare a son, and called his name Samson"* (v.24).

16

In the Hebrew tradition, the father was supposed to name the child, not the mother. I feel this is further evidence that Manoah did not step up to take his proper role as leader. This situation created an open invitation for problems to enter the home.

## A New Day

The name Samson means "little sun." I believe the woman saw her son's birth as the dawning of a new day for the people of God! The daylight of God's deliverance had come! The sunshine of divine liberty was intended to be manifest through this child.

**THE SUNSHINE OF DIVINE LIBERTY WAS INTENDED TO BE MANIFEST THROUGH THIS CHILD.**

Judges 13 closes by revealing, even as a young boy, the anointing of God was beginning to function in Samson's life. Scripture states, *"...the child grew, and the Lord blessed him. And the spirit of the Lord began to move him at times in the camp of Dan"* (vv.24-25).

Obviously, Samson began to recognize his great strength early in life—when God's Spirit began to "move him."

## Special Treatment?

You may ask, "If this family is out of order, how

could Samson have God's blessing and anointing?"

Remember, God's design for Samson was to "deliver Israel from Philistine bondage," and the Father's purpose would remain clear throughout his life. The family disorder, however, obviously impacted him.

One of the ways Samson may have been affected regards the use of discipline. Because of the supernatural circumstances surrounding his birth, Samson's parents may have treated him as a "special child." After all, an angel of God told them of his birth and purpose.

Perhaps they felt because their son was so unusual, he would automatically be born fully equipped with all the "godly characteristics" he needed—and discipline would not be necessary.

I'm not suggesting Samson's parents were not God-fearing people—there was no doubt they loved the Lord. Even today, a common mistake is to assume God is going to take care of certain responsibilities when they are clearly ours to handle. We are to raise our children in a godly manner. The Lord will not do that for us. He will help us, guide us, and grace us, but it is still our personal assignment!

*A COMMON MISTAKE IS TO ASSUME GOD IS GOING TO TAKE CARE OF CERTAIN RESPONSIBILITIES WHEN THEY ARE CLEARLY OURS TO HANDLE.*

## Set Apart

Being a parent is not a job for cowards or compromisers. It is a sacred responsibility.

Teaching our children to love, honor and fear God is not always an easy task, but it is one that can be accomplished with the Lord's help and encouragement. The long term dividends will be well worth the time and effort invested.

In the Old Testament, only two people had their birth foretold by an angel—Isaac and Samson. In the New Testament the same occurred with Jesus and John the Baptist.

What would become of this young man who was dedicated and set apart for God?

*When we pursue what we don't need, we receive what we don't want.*

– Al Gluchoski

# 2

# WHY PURSUE WHAT YOU DON'T NEED?

At the ripe old age of 18, Samsom decided to spread his wings and flex his muscles. By himself, he journeyed south to a Philistine city named Timnath.

As we will discover, this is more than a geographical "going down." It is also the beginning of a dramatic spiritual decline.

In this city, whose very name means "division," Samson begins to separate and divide from God. On his arrival, he catches a glimpse of a young Philistine woman and was instantly attracted to her.

Immediately, he rushed back home and exclaimed to his mother and father, *"I have seen a woman in Timnath of the daughters of the Philistines: now therefore get her for me to wife"* (Judges 14:2).

As you can imagine, Samson's parents were in a state of shock. They questioned, *"Is there never a woman among the daughters of thy brethren, or among all my people, that thou goest to take a wife of the uncircumcised Philistines?"* (Judges 14:3).

After all, this was the same son whom the angel prophesied would deliver Israel. Surely, this could not be part of God's covenant with His people!

**SAMSON IS ONLY A TEENAGER, YET HE IS APPARENTLY RUNNING THE HOUSE—USING INTIMIDATION TO MANIPULATE HIS PARENTS.**

## Who's in Charge?

The young man, however, is totally smitten by the looks of the woman and repeats to his father, *"Get her for me; for she pleaseth me well"* (v.3).

What we are seeing is a classic case of "the tail wagging the dog!" Samson is only a teenager, yet he is apparently running the house—using intimidation to manipulate his parents. Can it be we have a spoiled child on our hands? His words are almost threatening: *"Get her for me!"*

24

The fractures of disorder are beginning to surface in this family, especially since the father does exactly what Samson demanded, even knowing it was wrong. Manoah should have stood firm, but he submitted to his son's desires.

## The Voice of Authority

Some may ask, "Why is it so important to train children to obey their parents?"

The answer is clear. If you raise your child to have little regard for your voice of authority, when God speaks to them, they'll be in the habit of ignoring authority's voice. For such a child, disobedience to God will be as easy as insubordination to his parents. Once a pattern of rejecting authority is established, it's difficult to change.

> *ONCE A PATTERN OF REJECTING AUTHORITY IS ESTABLISHED, IT'S DIFFICULT TO CHANGE.*

In the final analysis, however, we can't continue to blame our parents for our lack of obedience. It is still our decision to either *obey* or *reject* the commands of God.

Such a destructive pattern was evident in the life of this young man.

## "Unequally Yoked"

Samson's parents were well aware of what their son

was ignoring: God forbids marriage between a believer and an unbeliever. Concerning the heathen, Moses declared to the Israelites, *"Neither shalt thou make marriages with them; thy daughter thou shalt not give unto his son, nor his daughter shalt thou take unto thy son"* (Deuteronomy 7:3).

Even today, the Word warns us: *"Be ye not unequally yoked together with unbelievers"* (2 Corinthians 6:14).

Samson brushed aside his parent's concerns and rashly pursued something he didn't need.

> **SAMSON BRUSHED ASIDE HIS PARENT'S CONCERNS AND RASHLY PURSUED SOMETHING HE DIDN'T NEED.**

## God's Will?

It is not clear why an immature Samson strayed into the enemy's camp to find a wife. Perhaps it was because, as historians point out, Hebrew women dressed quite modestly, while the Philistine women of the day were very scantily clad. Their religion even allowed for temple prostitutes.

God may have permitted this example to fulfill His purpose, but it was certainly not His will. The Lord never leads anyone into sin.

Samson *stubbornly* and *lustfully* chased this woman, regardless of the teaching of his parents—or God's law.

Think of it this way: An alcoholic husband is about to

leave home for the local bar. His wife begs him not to go there again. He tells her "leave me alone, That's where I'm headed!"

After pleading with him, she says "If you are going, will you at least pick up some bread on the way back?"

As you read this book, I believe you will see my point. God is going to use Samson to pick up some "Philistine bread" on the way home!

## *Ignoring the Consequences*

Reluctantly, Manoah and his wife consent to their son's wishes and make the journey to arrange the wedding. On the way, Samson leaves his parents to check out the vineyards of Timnath.

Why would he want to veer off course? Is it youthful curiosity? Perhaps, but he had no business being there. After all, he was a Nazarite, and if he ate the fruit of the vine he would be violating one of his vows.

**WHY WOULD HE WANT TO VEER OFF COURSE? IS IT YOUTHFUL CURIOSITY?**

Without question, his mother has warned him of the consequences all of his young life—yet when you chase something you're not supposed to have, compromise in other areas will always be the result.

Suddenly, in the vineyards, *"behold, a young lion*

27

*roared against him"* (v.5).

## Extraordinary Strength!

What happens next reveals the source of Samson's supernatural strength. *"And the spirit of the Lord came mightily upon him, and he rent him as he would have rent a kid, and he had nothing in his hand: but he told not his father or his mother what he had done"* (v.6).

What a picture! Samson is able to grab the lion by the hind legs and rip him in half! I know some NFL coaches who would have immediately signed him to a long-term contract!

*HE WAS ABLE TO TEAR AN ANIMAL LIMB FROM LIMB BECAUSE OF A SPECIAL ANOINTING FROM THE LORD!*

This was the first time Samson truly discovered his God-given physical power. Many scholars believe he was an ordinary man with extraordinary strength—not from working out or weight-lifting, but given this power directly from the Almighty. He was able to tear an animal limb from limb because of a special anointing from the Lord!

## A Sense of Shame

Yet, this young man is being trapped by compromise

—the result of sacrificing character and integrity for the purpose of pleasing his flesh. Perhaps he thought, "If I can have the girl, why can't I have the grapes?"

Why didn't Samson immediately tell his parents what he had done? Was he ashamed of killing the lion? I doubt it. There was nothing wrong with that feat—no vow or law had been broken. Rather, what Samson wanted to hide was eating the grapes of the vineyard.

**PERHAPS HE THOUGHT, "IF I CAN HAVE THE GIRL, WHY CAN'T I HAVE THE GRAPES?"**

At this point, there is still a sense of shame living in the young man, but soon that will also leave him. As we will see, the next time temptation is presented, disobedience will become easier.

Continuing on their journey, he and his parents *"went down, and talked with the woman; and she pleased Samson well"* (v.7). With the details of the wedding arranged, they returned home.

## "Turned Aside"

Soon the time arrived for Samson and his family to make the final trip to Timnath—for a lavish feast and the week-long marriage celebration.

On the way, when Samson came close to the spot where he had killed the animal, *"he turned aside to see the carcass of the lion: and, behold, there was a swarm of bees and honey in the carcass"* (v.8).

The phrase "turned aside" tells us that the vineyards were not on the pathway to Timnath. He had to willfully wander off the road to reach the vineyards. Samson didn't just stumble upon them—He veered off course and deliberately went there.

> **THIS IS ALWAYS SIN'S DESIGN FOR OUR LIVES; TO DISTRACT AND STEER US OFF THE RIGHT PATH BY ENTICING US TO PURSUE OUR OWN LUSTS.**

This is always sin's design for our lives; to distract and steer us off the right path by enticing us to pursue our own lusts.

## Broken Vows

When Samson discovers bees have nested in the carcass and made honey, perhaps he sees the honey as a reward for his conquest, the sweetness of his victory!

With no apparent hesitation, Samson scoops out some of the honey and has a meal. In doing this, he violates another aspect of the Nazarite vow by touching the dead body of the lion.

He then rejoins his parents and even offers them some of the honey, with no regard for the fact he has now defiled them with the substance of his disobedience. Again, he does not tell his parents how he obtained the honey (v.9) since that would reveal to them his breaking of the vow.

At this point, Samson has desecrated two of the four Nazarite vows and the wedding ceremony hasn't even started!

## His Own Ability?

As we continue the story, there is no indication Samson has seen the consequences for his sins—even though he has been told all his life what would happen if he broke those vows! He may have thought, "Perhaps God isn't all that concerned about my commitments. After all, I've broken two of them and nothing has happened to me yet! Look how powerfully I was anointed when I killed that lion! God was still with me, even then!"

*I BELIEVE SAMSON MISTAKENLY TOOK GOD'S MERCY AND LONGSUFFERING FOR A PERMISSION SLIP TO SKIP SCHOOL!*

I believe Samson mistakenly took God's mercy and longsuffering for a permission slip to skip school! Another danger: Samson started to think that God's anointing on him was actually his own ability and "It doesn't matter how I act, I can kill lions!"

Samson reached down, *"And he took thereof in his hands, and went on eating"* (v.9).

## It's Party Time!

Arriving in the city of Timnath, while his father busied himself with the final preparations for the celebration and ceremony, Samson threw a big *feast* (v.10)—as was the custom for young men in those days.

The Hebrew word for feast here is "mishteh" which means "a drinking party." Samson's regard for his vows have now been openly violated.

One of the sad aspects brought to light in this story is the fact Samson didn't have one Israelite friend attend his wedding—not even a best man! When the bride's family saw this, *"they brought thirty companions to be with him"* (v.11).

Could the reason be nobody likes to hang around an 18-year-old spoiled teen who always demands his own way?

**BEING A LEADER REQUIRES YOU TO RECEIVE SOUND ADVICE FROM A PERSON WHO HAS BEEN A LEADER THEMSELVES.**

## Ignoring Counsel

Being a leader requires you to receive sound advice from a person who has been a leader themselves. This was sadly lacking in Samson's life. "To lead" implies someone is following you. This is not the case here. Samson was a loner—acting independently of advice from others. The only counsel he seemed willing to follow was the promptings of the lust of his own flesh!

He ignored his parents advice and was now in a foreign land, partying with people he didn't really know. Even worse, he breaks the third Nazarite vow—taking strong drink.

## The Riddle

Surrounded by inebriated strangers, Samson decides to take advantage of the situation. He announces, "Men, I have a riddle I want you to solve. If anyone can figure it out, I'll give each of you a new garment."

Then he added, "But if you can't solve the riddle within seven days," by the end of the wedding celebration, "you each have to give me a new garment!"

They all agreed: "Put forth thy riddle, that we may hear it" (v.13).

Samson's brain-teaser concerned the killing of the lion and the honeycomb in its carcass. He thought, "They'll never figure this one out. I just got 30 new suits 'in the bag!'"

Here is what Samson challenged the guests to solve: *"Out of the eater came forth meat, and out of the strong came forth sweetness"* (v.14).

Samson must have confidently smiled to himself,

**HE ANNOUNCES, "MEN, I HAVE A RIDDLE I WANT YOU TO SOLVE. IF ANYONE CAN FIGURE IT OUT, I'LL GIVE EACH OF YOU A NEW GARMENT!"**

knowing he was the only person on earth who knew all the details.

## A Chance to Brag

Perhaps you wonder, "Why would Samson even give such a riddle?" After all, it seems a bit childish.

Put yourself in his shoes. Have you ever accomplished something outstanding you couldn't—or didn't—tell anyone about? Remember how you felt you would burst if you didn't share your story?

These heathen Philistines knew nothing of the Nazarite vow, and could care less if it were broken. So Samson took the opportunity to blow his own horn. He thought, "Here's my chance to boast about what I did to that lion!"

*IT WAS GOD'S ANOINTING, NOT SAMSON'S ABILITY, WHICH ALLOWED HIM TO KILL THE LION!*

However, there was a larger issue at stake. It was *God's anointing*, not Samson's ability, which allowed him to kill the lion!

Now he was using what God had accomplished for his own personal gain. The New Testament calls that "merchandising" the anointing. This is a clear misuse of the purpose for this awesome, divine power.

## Making "Merchandise"

Sorry to say, this same pattern continues. Scripture tells us that in the last days, *"And through covetousness shall they with feigned words make merchandise of you"* (2 Peter 2:3). To "make merchandise" simply means to take advantage of someone for your own profit and gain.

This was one of the reasons Lucifer sinned—and fell from heaven. The Bible records, *"By the multitude of thy merchandise they have filled the midst of thee with violence, and thou hast sinned: therefore I will cast thee as profane out of the mountain of God: and I will destroy thee, O covering cherub, from the midst of the stones of fire"* (Ezekiel 28:16).

**IN SAMSON'S SITUATION, WE ARE SEEING A VERY FLIPPANT ATTITUDE TOWARD THE PRECIOUS, HOLY ANOINTING.**

## Threatened with Death

In Samson's situation, we are seeing a very flippant attitude toward the precious, holy anointing.

As expected, the Philistines were stumped: *"And they could not in three days expound the riddle"* (Judges 14:14).

All the while, they threatened Samson's new bride with death—and how they would burn her father's house down (v.15) if she didn't entice him to reveal the answer to the riddle. Now, all Samson heard was, "You don't love me. You won't even tell me the answer!"

Day after day, she compelled him to share the secret —perhaps even using the threat of sexual abstinence to coerce Samson to tell her the answer. Protesting, he replies, *"Behold, I have not told it my father nor my mother, and shall I tell it thee?"* (v.16).

Finally, he succumbs to her persuasion.

Immediately, she runs to tell the Philistines.

## "Gutless Cowards"

*SAMSON FELT THAT IN THE TELLING OF HIS RIDDLE TO THOSE MEN, HIS WIFE HAD BEEN MORE INTIMATE WITH THEM THAN SHE HAD BEEN WITH HIM.*

The 30 young men "solved" the riddle and Samson realized he'd been tricked and betrayed!

It hurt him deeply. Greatly troubled, he said to them, *"If ye had not plowed with my heifer, ye had not found out my riddle"* (v.18).

Heifers (young female cows), were not used for plowing. Samson is bluntly saying, "You have used my wife wrongly, and you are gutless cowards for doing so!"

A heifer is also one that has not yet had sexual relations. Samson felt that in the telling of his riddle to those men, his wife had been more "intimate" with them then she had with him. The sting of this betrayal angered Samson beyond words—and if you are a Philistine, you don't want to get this guy upset with you!

## Paying Off His Bet

Samson rushes down to Ashkelon, and again under a powerful anointing, strength stirs within him and he kills 30 Philistines with his bare hands (v.19). He then takes their garments to pay off his bet.

*APPARENTLY, SAMSON THINKS IT IS MORE IMPORTANT TO PAY OFF HIS WAGER TO A GROUP OF UNGODLY PHILISTINES, THAN IT IS TO KEEP HIS COVENANT WITH ALMIGHTY GOD!*

Here's the problem. Not only were these men innocent, but in order to obtain their clothes, Samson must touch their dead bodies, which once more violates his Nazarite vow!

Apparently, Samson thinks it is more important to pay off his wager to a group of ungodly Philistines, than it is to keep his covenant with Almighty God!

Scripture refers to such a person as a man-pleaser— and we are warned of the consequences.

According to scripture, this is what caused Saul to lose his office and anointing as King of Israel. *"And Saul said unto Samuel, I have sinned: for I have transgressed* the commandment of the Lord, and thy words: because I feared the people, and obeyed their voice" (1 Samuel 15:24).

The apostle Paul writes: "...for if I yet pleased men, I should not be the servant of Christ" (Galatians 1:10).

## The Wrong Pursuit

What happened to Samson? He abruptly leaves the wedding celebration and heads home in anger, not knowing what would become of his "wife."

**WHEN WE PURSUE WHAT WE DON'T NEED, WE RECEIVE WHAT WE DON'T WANT!**

After all this, Samson loses what he compromised to get. What a lesson! When we pursue of what we don't need, we receive what we don't want!

When we chose to chase after an object of our lust instead of following God's plan, we will eventually break our godly commitments because they are now "in the way" of what we desire! They are no longer as important to us as what we are pursuing.

For example, one could say "I can no longer tithe because I have to pay off my credit card which I have charged over my limit." Our inordinate desires can create situations that become more pressing than our commitments to our Heavenly Father. These things may not seem overly troubling at first, but they are the foundation of compromise and it's trappings.

Here lies the danger. If we fail to restrict our fleshly desires in the small areas—when the temptation to commit adultery is presented—we'll already be in the habit of overlooking a godly standard of life.

Sin is always easier when it has become a routine. If we submit, we will be its slave.

> *SIN IS ALWAYS EASIER WHEN IT HAS BECOME A ROUTINE. IF WE SUBMIT, WE WILL BE ITS SLAVE.*

## Check Your Soil

Was it just carnal lust that caused Samson to desire and pursue this Philistine woman? Could it be Samson was seeking acceptance from the Philistines because God's people were just too boring for his youthful passions? I can hear him complaining, "The Philistines have all the fun and all I ever do is go to the temple."

I must admit that in my younger days as a Christian these were thoughts I occasionally experienced. Thankfully, I eventually matured in Christ and discovered true satisfaction and "fun" can only come from being what God has purposed you to be—and joyfully submitting to His plan for your life. Once that path is discovered, it creates an unstoppable passion in the pursuit of God's dream for your future!

When we run after things we don't need, frustration

is always the result. It becomes the soil out of which the weeds of anger, offense, bitterness and dissatisfaction begin to grow.

## A Future in Question

With his life in disarray, what would become of Samson—and the woman he was about to marry?

What was God's purpose in allowing these things to happen?

What lessons will we learn from Samson's troubling life?

*Whatever God anoints you to do, it is He, not you, who accomplishes the task.*

– Al Gluchoski

# 3

# BEYOND OUR STRENGTH

As I study the life experiences of Samson, my mind flashes back to a time when my world was totally focused on strength, agility and defeating an opponent!

During my junior year at West Virginia University, we were having a very poor football season, finishing the year with a 4-7 record. It certainly was not from lack of talent or poor coaching. Out of the junior and senior classes of the 1974 squad, over seventeen players signed NFL contracts. We simply did not play very well as a team.

Safe to say, towards the end of that season, most of the guys were thinking, "I just want to get this thing over with!"

The team was receiving a scouting report for one of the season's final games. Our attitude was not the best—we were just going through the motions of showing interest! I played center, so I wanted to know what kind of nose tackle the opposing team had.

When the scout began to describe my opponent, he simply said that he was an "overweight kid with baby-fat who had a hard time moving."

With such a report, I was not very motivated to prepare for a "classic battle" between two titans!

## A Brick Wall!

Game day arrived, yet I wasn't really "fired up" about facing this well-fed nose tackle.

After the kickoff, our team was on offense and I lined up for the first play. To my shock and amazement, Mr. Baby-Fat's arms were bigger than my legs, and they were definitely not fat!

*I SNAPPED THE BALL AND FIRED OFF TO BLOCK THIS GUY AND IT FELT LIKE HITTING A BRICK WALL.*

I snapped the ball and fired off to block this guy and it felt like hitting a brick wall. He was stronger than anybody I'd ever hit in my life! Along with that, he was quick and moved with great skill and agility. I knew I was in for a long day and I wasn't ready—mentally or physically. Even more,

I could have strangled the man who gave us that scouting report! Needless to say, it was not one of my better games.

I tried to fire myself up at halftime, but it just didn't work! We lost the game and I was embarrassed over how I had played. The season soon ended, but I didn't get over the sinking feeling I had experienced in that game.

## Time in the Weight Room

At the end of my junior year, the schedule for the following season was released and I saw that our first game was against Goliath and his team. (He was no longer referred to as Mr. Baby-Fat.)

When all the pre-season magazines came out, both Goliath and myself were picked as All-Stars. Talk about motivation! The summer before my senior year, I spent most of my days in the weight room. My goal was to

*DURING THOSE HOT MONTHS, I MUST ADMIT THAT FACING GOLIATH AGAIN WAS NEVER FAR FROM MY THINKING.*

make it to the NFL and I was no slouch in preparing for the task ahead!

During those hot months, I must admit that facing Goliath again was never far from my thinking.

Our senior team included a great bunch of guys. We

worked well together and encouraged each other daily. As we were preparing for our opening game, many on the squad would not let me forget my previous encounter with Goliath. The truth was, I didn't need to be reminded!

## "Hey Al!"

On game day, Tommy Bowden, a close friend and one of our wide receivers, said, "Hey Al, I read in an interview where Goliath (he used his real name) stated he didn't expect to have too much trouble with you. He said he handled you last year and things would be no different this time around."

I later discovered Tommy was just making up the story in order to motivate me. For some of my teammates, my encounter with Goliath was a game within the game!

**THE STADIUM WAS FILLED. THE REFEREE'S WHISTLE BLEW AND I WAS READY FOR A GAME I'LL NEVER FORGET.**

## Blocking Goliath!

The stadium was filled. The referee's whistle blew and I was ready for a contest I'll never forget. It soon became obvious we were in control of the game. I blocked Goliath extremely well.

On one pass play, I delivered a particularly hard shot to him. Our guard who saw the collision said, "Wow, Al, I've never seen a hit like that!"

We won the game 50-7 and what turned out to be a banner senior season had begun. Coach Bobby Bowden even came out with several statements in the media as to "the outstanding job Gluchoski did in handling their nose tackle."

## "The Zone"

I'm not relating this story to convince you of the kind of player I was back then or to brag. The reason I share this is because I know that day I played beyond my own talents and abilities.

*I DIDN'T KNOW WHAT "THE ANOINTING" WAS AT THE TIME, BUT LOOKING BACK, I AM CONVINCED IT WAS RESTING ON ME DURING THAT GAME!*

Yes, I was prepared and ready, but it was not only my natural skills which were demonstrated in that game. It was as if I had been empowered by God Himself. I didn't know what "the anointing" was at the time, but looking back, I am convinced it was resting on me during that game!

The term many athletes have used to describe such a

feeling is being "in the zone." In retrospect, I firmly believe the zone I was in was created by the grace and power of Almighty God!

## It's "Him!"

Samson had many more powerful encounters than my football story. His error was not recognizing that it was God's Spirit upon him. It lead to pride and his eventual destruction.

> **REMEMBER, WHATEVER GOD ANOINTS YOU TO DO, IT IS HE, NOT YOU, WHO ACCOMPLISHES THE TASK.**

Remember, whatever God anoints you to do, it is *He*, not you, who accomplishes the task.

In case you're wondering who "Goliath" was in my story. His name is Joe Klecko—who went on to become an All-Pro defensive lineman with the New York Jets.

In my humble opinion, Joe should be inducted into the NFL Hall of Fame. He was a tremendous, devastating athlete and played in the NFL for many years at an All-Star level.

## Obeying God

Now, as a minister and evangelist, I fully understand the difference between our own power and God's.

Recently, during the last night of a crusade I was

conducting, people came to the altar to receive prayer for healing. The line was fairly long and, truthfully, after preaching I was very tired. I felt no unusual anointing, no power or any special presence of God.

That night, I walked up to a young boy who appeared to be about ten years old. Obeying the scriptural command to *"lay hands on the sick, and they shall recover"* (Mark 16:18), I prayed for him.

A few days after returning home, I received a call from the pastor of the church.

*"Al, Do You Remember The Young Man You Prayed For On The Last Night Of The Meeting?"*

"Al, do you remember the young man you prayed for on the last night of the meeting?"

I thought for a moment and could visualize the young lad in my mind's eye.

"Well, the boy's parents brought him to my office to show me what had happened," continued the excited minister.

## New Toes!

I learned the boy's toes were gone—so he had to wear special shoes to help him walk correctly.

The morning after that healing service, the young boy

awoke to find that his toes had grown to such an extent he could no longer fit into his corrective shoes. Overjoyed, mom and dad took him to show the pastor what a miracle God had performed!

When I had prayed for their son, I had no idea of his need. I was not exercising "toe-growing faith!" Yes, I was believing for his healing, but I was unaware of the specifics of his condition. In other words, all I did was lay hands on him as the Word commands. God was the one who was bringing healing!

I was thrilled to hear of this young man's faith and testimony—a living witness to the fact it is the Lord, not you or me, who truly does the work!

As we return to the story of Samson, we begin to see how it is not man's strength, but God's purpose which really matters.

# *Revenge is reserved for God's use, not ours.*

– Al Gluchoski

# 4

# Vengeance is Mine – but Use Me Lord!

Who could blame Samson for leaving Timnath in a huff when his bride shared the secret of his riddle with the Philistine men?

Still, he considered the woman to be his wife. After his temper cooled, he decided to return to the scene of the marriage and make amends. He thought the time was right, especially since it was the busy season of the wheat harvest.

Samson had no idea the girl's father considered him a deserter from the family and had given his daughter *"to his companion, whom he had used as his friend"* (Judges 14:20). The Philistine-chosen "best man" was now the woman's husband!

## Learning the Truth

In Hebrew custom, the type of marriage which was arranged is called a "sadiqa-marriage." The wife still lived with her parents and the husband visited for the purpose of marital relations.

As was the practice in those days, Samson brought a kid goat as a present to her father, then said, *"I will go in to my wife into the chamber. But her father would not suffer him to go in"* (Judges 15:1).

*ONCE MORE, SAMSON'S ANGER FLARED. HE EXCLAIMED, "THIS TIME I HAVE EVERY RIGHT TO GET EVEN WITH THE PHILISTINES!"*

At that moment, Samson learned the truth. His father-in-law explained, "I thought you hated her, so I gave her to your companion." Then he offered to Samson the hand of his younger daughter in marriage (v.2).

Once more, Samson's anger flared. He exclaimed, "This time I have every right to get even with the Philistines!" He began plotting to retaliate—to cause them harm.

Samson was discovering the true character of these people and his frustration was about to be vented.

## Fields of Fire!

In an act of revenge, Samson caught 300 foxes and tied their tails together in pairs. That act alone required divine strength! He then placed a lighted torch in the knot of each pair of foxes and let them loose in the cornfields of the Philistines!

I can imagine Samson receiving a nasty letter from the Philistine Animal Rights Association! This act of vengeance burned up the corn, the stalks, the vineyards and the olive trees.

*I CAN IMAGINE SAMSON RECEIVING A NASTY LETTER FROM THE PHILISTINE ANIMAL RIGHTS ASSOCIATION!*

It was a crippling blow to the Philistine economy. Theirs was an agricultural society and their stock market crashed because Samson did this during harvest season!

Along with the economic devastation, this was also an insult to the Philistine god Dagon, their god of grain and harvest!

When the Philistines discovered what Samson had done, in retaliation they killed his bride and father-in-law with fire. The cycle of vengeance had started, and—as we will see—it perpetuated.

# Revenge! Revenge!

Now it was Samson's turn. Angered by the killing of his "wife," He told them, *"Though you have done this, yet will I be avenged of you, and after that I will cease"* (Judges 17:7).

In other words, "I'll have my revenge, and then it will be over!"

Seething with rage, Samson kills a large number of Philistines with his bare hands! The Bible records, *"...he smote them hip and thigh with a great slaughter"* (v.8)—he tore them apart limb from limb and piled them in a heap as a memorial to his victory!

SEETHING WITH RAGE, SAMSON KILLS A LARGE NUMBER OF PHILISTINES WITH HIS BARE HANDS!

Samson escapes into Judah, but as we know, man's vengeance is never fully satisfied.

Next, it was the Philistine's turn. They deployed at least 1,000 warriors to Judah to find and destroy Samson. I'm sure they thought this was more than enough to capture one man!

The inhabitants of Judah were God's people, yet they were fearful of the Philistines. They asked the approaching army, "Why are you coming against us?"

They responded: *"To bind Samson are we come up,*

*to do to him as he hath done to us"* (v.10).

## Reacting in Fear

The men of Judah were caught in a tricky political situation. Since they were ruled by the Philistines, they didn't want any trouble. So they called together 3,000 men to look for Samson—in order to turn him over to the Philistines.

Yes, 3000 men to capture one guy! I suppose they didn't want to take any chances.

Judah's citizens were obviously reacting in fear of the Philistines, but it's evident they had little respect for Samson as a leader of Israel.

They should have been thrilled to hear of his conquest over the enemies of God, but instead it filled them with anxiety and trepidation.

Remember, it was their sin that had placed them in bondage to the Philistines in the first place—and iniquity apparently also removed their courage and desire to fight for freedom. The men of Judah had grown too comfortable with their bondage. Their desire for freedom was gone!

> *JUDAH'S CITIZENS WERE OBVIOUSLY REACTING IN FEAR OF THE PHILISTINES, BUT IT'S EVIDENT THEY HAD LITTLE RESPECT FOR SAMSON AS A LEADER OF ISRAEL.*

## No Friends

Samson's compromise caused him to make enemies on both sides of the fence. He not only had Philistine foes, but now even God's people were out to get him—a combined total of 4,000 if you're counting!

As judge of Israel, he should have been a leader of men, gaining their respect and admiration. Instead, Samson had accomplished his exploits all by himself, with no help from anyone in Israel. There was no inner circle of friends—no one to receive wisdom and council from—no one to speak into his life.

*AN UNWILLINGNESS TO BE TEACHABLE AND RECEIVE FROM OTHERS IS A SIGN OF PRIDE.*

An unwillingness to be teachable and receive from others is a sign of pride. This is likely the reason the men of Judah had so little respect for him as their leader.

## "What Are You Doing?"

They found Samson in a cave, high on the rock of Etam. The name means "place of wild beasts." It makes me think Samson was resting with his own kind!

The men of Judah questioned him: "Don't you know that the Philistines are our rulers! What are you doing to us?"

Samson's defense was, *"As they did unto me, so have I done unto them"* (v.11).

## What Irony!

His Israeli captors let Samson know they were going to tie him up and deliver him over to the Philistines.

Samson only suggests, "Swear unto me that you won't kill me yourselves!"

**HIS OWN COUNTRYMEN WERE SAYING, "WE WON'T KILL YOU, BUT WE ARE GOING TO TIE YOU UP AND HAND YOU TO THE MOST VILE, CRUEL PEOPLE ON THE FACE OF THE EARTH."**

They agree, but let him know he would be handed over to the enemy.

What irony! His own countrymen were saying, "We won't kill you, but we are going to tie you up and hand you to the most vile, cruel people on the face of the earth. They want you dead worse than anybody!   Don't worry though, we'll be praying for you Samson!  After all, we are your brothers in the Lord!"

I think you get the picture.

Fear and sin have caused the men of Judah to lose courage, while Samson's driving force is vengeance—and would remain so until the day of his death.

## Inner Turmoil

Samson's conquest of the Philistines had begun, yet it was triggered by lust, offence and retribution. What may seem to be the right actions have been initiated by the wrong reasons.

Often, we can cover up bitterness and anger by doing what is outwardly "the right thing" and give the appearance we are God's hero of the hour! However, what matters most is the motivation of our heart.

**THE INNER TURMOIL WHICH WAS DRIVING SAMSON WILL ALSO BE THE CAUSE OF HIS EVENTUAL DOWNFALL.**

As we will see, the inner turmoil which was driving Samson will also be the cause of his eventual downfall. It was his lust for a Philistine woman that started this "adventure"—and will become one of the major reasons for the loss of his powerful anointing.

At this point, however, the special touch of God's Spirit was still active and powerful, despite the poor stewardship Samson had shown.

## A Warring Spirit

Revenge is reserved for God's use, not ours. We have a responsibility to bless those who persecute us and pray for those (not prey on those) who despitefully use us.

You and I are to pray that the light of the Gospel will shine on those who have offended us. If vengeance is needed, let God do His job!

I realize the Lord is using Samson here to destroy the Philistines and set His people free. However, it was Samson's lust and stubbornness which launched him into this Philistine conquest, and his warring spirit was being fanned by the flame of revenge.

Again, there are right actions with wrong reasons. We must recognize that sin of any kind must never be used as the driving factor to accomplish a desired result. If so, it will become a seed of corruption producing an eventual harvest of death.

> *WE MUST RECOGNIZE THAT SIN OF ANY KIND MUST NEVER BE USED AS THE DRIVING FACTOR TO ACCOMPLISH A DESIRED RESULT.*

## The Folly of Deceit

Have you ever made the mistake of lying to a friend concerning something you did? In most cases, you compound the problem by adding other lies along the way in order to maintain the so-called "truth" of your story? It can become quite messy!

Eventually the *real* story comes to the surface and we

feel like fools.

Similarly, we all know someone who has told the same fabricated story for so long they actually begin to believe it as truth!

Here's the point: how you enter a situation is how it will be maintained and completed. Let's be sure our actions have the right motives.

## On Campus

**THERE'S ALWAYS VALUE IN DOING THE RIGHT THING, EVEN WHEN YOU THINK NO ONE IS LOOKING.**

There's always value in doing the right thing, even when you think no one is looking. Let me share one example.

During my college football days at West Virginia, I made some great friends. In our senior year, my roommate was Dave Van Halanger who is now a Hall of Fame Strength Coach at the University of Georgia.

Dave and I gave our hearts to the Lord the same night in our freshman year and we've been close friends since that time.

Our next door neighbor was Tommy Bowden, who is now the head coach at Clemson University. His dad Bobby, was our coach at WVU before he became a legend at Florida State.

## "Probing Questions"

One day, Tommy stopped by my room and we decided to play a trick on Dave. Tommy was going to hide in the other room and when Dave came home, I would ask him leading questions about Tommy—with the goal being to embarrass Dave.

When he arrived I mentioned that Tommy had just left, and my "probing questions" began. Of course, my inquiries were tailor-made to make Tommy look bad.

Before long Dave was uttering phrases such as, "Yeah, Tommy sure is stupid for having done that!"

*BEFORE LONG, DAVE WAS UTTERING PHRASES SUCH AS, "YEAH, TOMMY SURE IS STUPID FOR HAVING DONE THAT!"*

Well, our plan worked like a charm, and in the middle of one of Dave's comments, out popped Tommy from behind the door. Needless to say, Dave felt about two inches tall!

Tommy and I cracked up— feeling we really got one over on our good friend Dave. But this wasn't the end of the story.

## "Crazy Tommy!"

A few weeks went by and the joke we played was

forgotten; at least I thought it was!

I came to my room from class one afternoon and Dave was there by himself. He told me Tommy had just left and had been talking incessantly about his dream of someday being a head football coach.

Of course, Dave's tone seemed to be implying, "Crazy Tommy is at it again!"

Well, I joined right in, agreeing, "That little goofball doesn't ever shut up, does he? All he ever talks about is how he's gonna be a head coach someday."

**THIS WAS MY "WATERGATE!" MY UNKIND WORDS WERE NOW FOREVER BURNED INTO "CASSETTE ETERNITY."**

Dave continued and so did my mouth! Soon, I realized he was up to something—and he was. Dave had secretly been recording our entire conversation on tape.

This was my "Watergate!" My unkind words were now forever burned into "cassette eternity." I was caught!

"Dave, please don't ever play that tape to Tommy!"

He just grinned from ear to ear—enjoying the sweet taste of revenge.

Blackmail was now a sword swinging over my head!

The Bible tells us, *"...for whatsoever a man soweth, that shall he also reap"* (Galatians 6:7). Now I was experiencing the harvest of some unholy seeds I had planted, and it was a hard lesson to learn.

As it turned out, Dave never did play that tape to Tommy—at least I don't think he did!

## Beyond Coaching

Today, Tommy Bowden is one of college football's premier head coaches. He was outstanding at Tulane University before moving on to Clemson.

Along with his dad Bobby, he will most likely be remembered as one of the sport's best. However, even more laudable than his coaching skills, Tommy is one of the finest Christian men you will ever meet.

*EVEN MORE LAUDABLE THAN HIS COACHING SKILLS, TOMMY IS ONE OF THE FINEST CHRISTIAN MEN YOU WILL EVER MEET.*

Dave Van Halanger has also made a lasting mark in the world of college football—as the strength coach at WVU, Florida State, and now the University of Georgia. He was recently inducted into the Hall of Fame for his work as a strength and conditioning coach. The NFL also named him as "Strength Coach of the Year"—no small accomplishment.

I am thrilled to say that many of today's NFL stars were influenced by the Christian life Coach Van has demonstrated daily before them. His zeal for the Lord

Jesus Christ is unquenchable and very contagious! Hundreds of young men have made decisions for Jesus because of his example. Only eternity will reveal the impact Tommy Bowden and Dave Van Halanger have made for God's Kingdom. I am proud and thankful to call them my friends.

## A Question of Offense

"Getting even" is a natural emotional response. It can either be done in good fun—as in the college pranks I described—or be taken to an extreme, as we find in the case of Samson.

**"GETTING EVEN" IS A NATURAL EMOTIONAL RESPONSE.**

Once, when ministering in a church, I preached a message dealing with guarding yourself from the poison of being offended. The sermon was well received and I could sense it was helping those in the congregation.

When the service was over, I walked to the lobby of the church and noticed quite a few people were purchasing the tape of that night's message. Just then, a woman walked up to me and asked this question: "Al, you said in your sermon we had to forgive those who have offended us. What do you do if the same person keeps repeating the offence over and over, even after you've forgiven them?"

Attempting to soften my answer, I replied, "Well, Jesus says we must forgive seventy times seven which equals 490 times. I guess after 490 you can stop!"

My light-hearted response brought a smile to her face, but soon I *met* her problem.

## Out of Control!

Approaching me was an extremely angry man who screamed, "How dare you say it's wrong to be offended! Jesus was offended at the money changers in the temple. Nehemiah was offended at the broken down walls of Jerusalem..." He went on and on, rampaging at the top of his voice. It drew the attention of everyone in the building.

*Approaching me was an extremely angry man who screamed, "How dare you say it's wrong to be offended!"*

I looked at the embarrassed woman and could tell by her expression this man was the problem she had been referring to!

Trying to calm him down, I attempted to convince the man he had misunderstood what I was saying in the message, but he just kept screaming, "I never misunderstand anything!"

I didn't know whether to cast the devil out of him or react in the flesh! As he continued his angry outburst, I wondered if I was going to have to physically defend myself.

## Poisoned!

The ushers finally arrived on the scene and literally dragged this guy away while he was still hollering! The woman apologized profusely for the actions of her husband. She shared how "her problem" becomes offended at literally *everything.* That night he was offended with the "Don't Get Offended" message!

Somehow, he was infected with the "poison of offense" and it was obviously controlling his life—the driving force of his words and actions.

> SOMEHOW, HE WAS INFECTED WITH THE "POISON OF OFFENSE" AND IT WAS OBVIOUSLY CONTROLLING HIS LIFE.

The very message that could have helped him most was rejected because he saw and heard it through poisoned eyes and ears.

## A False Perspective

This is similar to what happened in Samson's life. Offense and revenge were the over-riding emotions in his conquest of the Philistines.

His actions appeared to be right—and they were certainly heroic! However, his perception of the need for obedience was affected by the force of vengeance operating inside. Obeying his Nazarite vows lost their importance because he perceived the end justified the means.

The man who confronted me believed "he was right." He even used scripture in an attempt to validate his point!

The problem is that an offended, vengeful person sees everything through a filter of false perspective. It causes the individual to wear "fogged up" glasses when perceiving the truth of God's Word. Someone who is offended is, in reality, rolling out the welcome mat for deception and its consequences.

As we will see, Samson's desire for retaliation and revenge would only compound his crisis.

*Your tomorrow, and the future of those you love, is too important to be sacrificed on the altar of pride.*

– Al Gluchoski

**5**

# THE PERIL
# OF PRIDE

Cornered in a cave by the men of Judah, Samson was bound with ropes and presented to the army of the Philistines. Perhaps we should say he "allowed" them to tie him up.

What we see next is one of the most awesome examples of God's anointing and power ever displayed by man! As the Philistines shouted and charged after Samson, the Spirit of God came on him and the ropes melted off his body—as if burned by fire (Judges 15:14).

In that moment, Samson found a fresh, moist jawbone of a donkey. With this as his only weapon, he killed

1,000 of the attacking Philistines.

What a scene it must have been. One man, plus God's mighty anointing, vanquishes an entire army! Sign this fellow up as your middle linebacker!

I can't help wondering what "Philistine soldier number 1,000" must have thought after 999 of his buddies had fallen to this *one* God-empowered man. Wow!

In the process, however, Samson committed one more grievous error. By picking up the jawbone, he touched an animal's dead body and again violated his Nazarite vow.

**BY PICKING UP THE JAWBONE, HE TOUCHED AN ANIMAL'S DEAD BODY AND AGAIN VIOLATED HIS NAZARITE VOW.**

## An Act of Heroism!

Some may question, "But what else could he have done?"

Remember, it was the anointing on him that allowed Samson to destroy the Philistines, *not* the jawbone. Try using such a weapon against 1,000 battle-ready men *without* the anointing and see what happens!

Of course, it takes outstanding courage for one individual to face such a vast army on the attack. Without doubt, this was great heroism – the kind of faith and action that will put you in the Hall of Fame. Next to the miracles of Jesus, this may be the most heroic act ever displayed by a human being. However, the fact remains: Samson violated his Nazarite vow.

Please don't miss the message. It was God's anointing, not the jawbone that defeated the enemy.

## Worth Singing About

Samson was so overjoyed, he began to sing and shout his own praises! Scholars believe the words found in Judges 15:16 are actually a song of rhyme Samson boastfully sang. One version of the scripture says,

> *With the jawbone of a donkey, I have killed 1,000 men.*
> *With the jawbone of a donkey I've made donkeys out of them!*

Today, we'd probably call this a rap song!

Here's our champion, now bragging about his exploits. He even magnifies the fact he used a jawbone to do the job—something he wasn't supposed to touch.

*I BELIEVE WE ARE SEEING SAMSON AT THE HEIGHT OF PRIDE AND ARROGANCE.*

I believe we are seeing Samson at the height of pride and arrogance. He is taking personal credit for what God's anointing has accomplished—like the person who prays, "Not thy will but mine be done!"

## A Troubling Pattern

After the massacre, Samson discarded the jawbone and named the place *Ramath-lehi* (Judges 15:17), which carries the meaning, "the lifting up of the jawbone."

> **"EVEN THOUGH I BROKE MY VOW, I STILL DEFEATED THOSE PHILISTINES. MY CONDUCT DOESN'T MATTER, JUST LOOK AT THE RESULTS I'VE BEEN GETTING."**

In Bible times, names were given as memorials to the event which occurred at a particular location. Samson named the site after the object he was not supposed to touch. It was as if he were defiantly saying, "Even though I broke my vow, I still defeated those Philistines! My conduct doesn't matter, just look at the results I've been getting."

Once more, we see a troubling pattern revealing a low regard for God's standards. It's an attitude which shouts, "I can do this on my own. I don't really need God's help."

## A Stamp of Approval?

Samson was now convinced it was his own ability which was bringing results, not Jehovah's touch.

We need to realize the Father's anointing on an individual is not always His stamp of approval on a person's conduct. Remember, God's intent for Samson was to "deliver Israel out of the hands of the Philistines," and God's purpose will always be accomplished!

I believe this begins to shed light on why some Christian leaders today may seem to be getting away with less than honorable behavior. God's longsuffering can "allow" a person to act in an improper manner, yet the gifting of that individual is still working to save, heal and set people free! This type of conduct, however, is poor stewardship of the Lord's wonderful gifting and anointing.

> *WE NEED TO REALIZE THE FATHER'S ANOINTING ON AN INDIVIDUAL IS NOT ALWAYS HIS STAMP OF APPROVAL ON A PERSON'S CONDUCT.*

As we discover in the case of the man in Matthew 25:28, what we use unwisely will be taken from us and given to someone who will use the gift correctly.

Unless the sin stops, the results will eventually be tragic.

## Where's the Repentance?

After this amazing conquest over the Philistines, Samson is exhausted and "dying" of thirst!

Only after reaching this point of weakness and severe need does Samson finally call on God. He cries, *"Thou hast given this great deliverance into the hand of thy servant: and now shall I die for thirst, and fall into the hand of the uncircumcised?"* (v.18).

He seems to be giving the Lord credit and even calls himself God's servant, but is he truly sincere? Is this just a prayer of desperation with little repentance attached?

I've met those who are sorry they got caught—not sorry for what they did!

> *I'VE MET THOSE WHO ARE SORRY THEY GOT CAUGHT— NOT SORRY FOR WHAT THEY DID!*

Regardless, God answered Samson's request by opening up a spring out of the ground. He drank its cool, clear water and was miraculously re-energized.

## Water from the Jaw

Scripture records, *"God clave an hollow place that was in the jaw, and there came water thereout; and when he had drunk, his spirit came again, and he revived: wherefore he called the name thereof Enhakkore, which is in Lehi unto this day"* (v.19).

Some have mistakenly concluded God had the water come out of the jawbone he used to slay the Philistines. No. The "jaw" means the place Lehi, not the animal's jaw. If God used the jawbone for the source of water, it would cause Samson to break his vow again. The water simply poured out of a pocket in the ground at Lehi. The final words of verse 19 tell us the spring is still there to this day.

## Blinded by Pride

After Samson is refreshed, he names the place *Enhakkore* which means, "The spring of him that cried out."

I don't want to be over-critical of our hero, but Samson still had lessons to learn. In naming the location after himself, he is saying, "I prayed and the water came out. My great faith resulted in this spring."

*PRIDE WILL BLIND US TO THE FACT IT IS THE LORD WHO ANSWERS OUR PRAYER!*

It sounds like pride to me!

The keys which open God's door are prayer and faith. Pride, however, will blind us to the fact it is the Lord who answers our prayer!

To be blunt, he called the spring "Samson's Well." If he were in today's tourism business, there would probably be a charge of $20 a visit!

## The Problems Compound

What may seem surprising is the fact God still

responded to Samson plea, even though he behaved so dreadfully. What is the reason? God's purpose and desire was to set His people free from Philistine bondage– and Samson happens to be God's man for the job.

Samson sees no cause for repentance, though it is desperately needed!

### SAMSON SEES NO CAUSE FOR REPENTANCE, THOUGH IT IS DESPERATELY NEEDED!

## A Missed Opportunity

Let's not forget the 3,000 men of Judah who turned Samson over to the Philistines. Remember, they've been carefully watching the dramatic series of events.

What an opportunity for Samson and Israel this might have been. After killing the 1,000 Philistines, Samson could have turned to the Israelites and exclaimed, "Look at the great victory God has given us today! He has anointed me to be your judge and leader. Through His grace and calling, I have been chosen as God's tool of deliverance from Philistine bondage as He demonstrated here so clearly! Let us unite, and we will become a nation of God's power and might in the earth. Join up with me, and the same anointing God has outpoured on me will also be given to you."

That very scenario happened to David's mighty men as recorded in 1 Chronicles 11.

Instead we hear, "'I' have slain 1000 men! 'I' prayed and water came out!"

The 3,000 men of Judah must have gone away shaking their heads at what they had witnessed. The very act which could have united and solidified God's people was used to display human pride and selfishness. Samson remained a "lone ranger" instead of becoming a true leader of God's people.

Yet, despite all his shortcomings, the Bible says, *"...he judged Israel in the days of the Philistines twenty years"* (Judges 15:20).

## Nothing is Hidden

As we read this story, it is transparent how Samson's personal flaws are being placed on public display. His sin is not only affecting him, it is now impacting others as well.

> **THERE'S NO SUCH THING AS "HIDDEN SIN" WHAT YOU ARE ON THE INSIDE WILL EVENTUALLY BE MADE MANIFEST ON THE OUTSIDE.**

There's no such thing as "hidden sin." What you are on the inside will eventually be made manifest on the outside. Jesus says, *"For there is nothing covered, that shall not be revealed; neither hid, that shall not be known"* (Luke 12:2).

The "covered" things Jesus is referring to is the hypocrisy and sin of the Pharisees. If hidden sin is a problem for you, don't keep repeating the transgression and trust God's love will continue to cover it up. Stop now! Repent before your life (and the lives of others) is affected.

Your tomorrow, and the future of those you love, is too important to be ruined by pride.

## A Tough Lesson

My first (and most memorable) lesson in humility came when I was in the sixth grade.

Our grammar school had a varsity basketball team limited to seventh and eighth graders. No students, other than "upperclassmen," were ever placed on the varsity team. However, one of my childhood friends and I were the first sixth graders to receive the honor.

*THE EXCITEMENT DEVELOPED INTO A SERIOUS CASE OF PRIDE—WHICH BEGAN TO BE DEMONSTRATED IN NOT-SO-SUBTLE WAYS.*

Needless to say, we were thrilled with our accomplishment!

In my case, the excitement developed into a serious case of pride—which began to be demonstrated in not-so-subtle ways.

When friends would ask me, "Hey Al, can you come over and play after school?" my response would always be, "I can't because we have *Varsity* basketball practice today." The emphasis was, of course, on

82

"varsity" practice.

I wanted everyone to know this hot-shot sixth grader was on the "big boy's" team!

## The Class Trip

After a short period of time, every response I made to any question was always marked with some reference to the fact I was on the varsity. My friends would ask, "Hey Al, would you like to sit with us for lunch." I'd reply, "Sorry, the *Varsity* players always sit over here!"

**LOOKING BACK, I DON'T KNOW HOW MY CLASSMATES COULD STAND TO BE AROUND ME.**

Looking back, I don't know how my classmates could stand to be around me.

My teacher, Miss Nesbihal, because she cared, decided to nip this situation in the bud! One day in school, with everyone present, she began to tell the students about a class field trip the sixth graders were going to take. She made it sound like it would be the most exciting trip in the world! Then she explained we would be assigned specific seats on the bus and we must sit together in pairs.

Next, she read aloud the names of all the student pairings, but my name was the only one she didn't announce.

Immediately, I raised my hand and said, "Miss Nesbihal, my name was not mentioned."

She looked me right in the eyes and gave this response: "The reason, Mr. Gluchoski, is because no one wants to sit next to a conceited, stuck up person like yourself. Plus we all figured you couldn't come on the trip because the *Varsity* has practice that day!"

## Serious Adjustments

Ouch! I will never forget the sting of her words. It seemed as if the entire class applauded and cheered as I fell flat on my emotional face! It didn't take me long to make some seriously needed adjustments.

From that day to this, I have never forgotten the importance of remaining humble. You need such chastising when you start to believe you are the next best thing since sliced bread!

If only Samson had learned this lesson!

*What we practice
on a consistent basis
develops and
dominates our
behavior.*

– Al Gluchoski

**6**

# THE STRONGHOLD TAKES CONTROL!

Some people just can't seem to stay out of trouble—and Samson was no exception.

Here was the leader of Israel, traveling down to Gaza, the capital city of the Philistines. And he certainly wasn't on a soul-saving mission! Scripture records he *"saw there an harlot, and went in unto her"* (Judges 16:1).

How disappointing. What seemed to be a moment of repentance in the previous chapter, did not last very long. His actions with the woman were not a specific violation of his Nazarite vow, rather a blatant disregard for the Law of God.

The word Gaza is significant as it means "place of the stronghold."

## The Small Things

Looking back, we have seen Samson separate from the Lord, override the check of the Holy Spirit, be disrespectful and disobedient to his parents, compromise his beliefs and display stubbornness, pride and lust. All these are elements of the stronghold that is about to take control of his life.

The drinking party at his wedding in Timnath was only an early step. Now we see his troubles multiplying.

> **WE MUST HANDLE THE SMALL ISSUES IN OUR LIVES BEFORE THEY ESCALATE AND DOMINATE OUR VERY EXISTENCE!**

This is a powerful example of why we must handle the small issues in our lives before they escalate and dominate our very existence!

## Who's in Control?

People have called alcoholism a "disease." Sorry, cancer is a disease; so is leukemia. Alcoholism, however, does *not* belong in that category. To call it a disease implies you have nothing to do with its onset.

Alcoholism begins as a lack of self-control that is demonstrated by your flesh after you have your first sip of beer or wine. Your carnal man begs for more and you cave in. You then keep allowing the flesh to yield to the craving until it finally takes total control.

# The "Little Foxes"

In my younger days, before I knew the Lord, I never saw a bottle of wine, a can of beer or a shot of tequila jump off the bar and into someone's mouth on it's own. A six-pack of beer does not open the refrigerator door and pour itself for you!

Full blown alcoholism may seem like a disease because of the damage it inflicts on the mind and body, but its onset is simply caused by the lust of the individual who is now addicted! If the issues were addressed properly in the early stages, it would never have developed into such a devastating bondage.

In Samson's case, the "little foxes" have grown up and are now controlling his life.

# At the Gates

The Gazites heard Samson was in town and they waited for him all night at the entrance to the city. Their plan was to kill him when he awoke and left town the next morning (v.2).

Samson, however, leaving the prostitute behind, rose up at midnight and went out to the city gates.

There, at the entrance to Gaza, he *"took the doors of the gate of the city, and the two posts, and went away with them, bar and all, and put them upon his shoulders, and carried them up to the top of an hill that is before Hebron"* (v.3).

## "I'm in Charge!"

What a feat!—especially since Hebron is 38 miles from Gaza! Samson carried the huge wooden, brass-covered gates with posts and crossbar over *uphill* terrain for most of those long miles.

Let me explain why I believe Samson did this. The gates of a city represent its authority—in this case the power of the headquarters of the Philistines.

In a mighty show of strength, Samson was saying, "I have possession and control of the authority over your capital city, therefore, I control all you Philistines!"

Even more, as he slammed down the gates and faced Hebron—a city of Judah—he was probably boasting to the Israelites, "I did this by myself. I didn't need your help!"

This was likely an "in your face" to the men of Judah for turning him over to the 1,000 Philistines when they were at Lehi.

## The Presence

You may wonder, "What happened to the Philistines who were waiting for Samson at the entrance to the city?"

Did they flee in terror when they saw Samson? Did his reputation precede him and scare them off? I don't think so. They were not hesitant or afraid to wait, while plotting to kill him. After all, these men were trained warriors—intimidatiors, not cowards.

I'm sure they were not asleep. The noise of gates being

ripped out of the ground would wake up even the most exhausted Philistine!

I believe when they encountered Samson at midnight, it wasn't what they "saw," rather what they *felt* that frightened them. Perhaps when they looked at Samson, they sensed a *Presence* on him they did not understand. Remember, it was the anointing of God "to deliver Israel from the Philistines."

*THE NOISE OF GATES BEING RIPPED OUT OF THE GROUND WOULD WAKE UP EVEN THE MOST EXHAUSTED PHILISTINE!*

They fled from the Presence of that anointing! These men left because they thought Dagon must be calling them to another place of "ministry" — excuse the humor!

What is almost unbelievable is that Samson was still anointed, even after being with the harlot of Gaza! That's hard for our human minds to comprehend, but whether we understand it or not, he was still blessed with divine strength. Just ask those gates!

## The Wrong Alliance

In looking at this incident, I believe there's a much deeper meaning. As I mentioned at the beginning of this chapter, the name Gaza means "stronghold" and the gates represent, "the authority" of the city.

In addition, the word Hebron carries the meaning "alliance—a joining together—a union."

Combining these together, when Samson took the gates of Gaza and carried them uphill to face Hebron, it is showing us he has "joined together, made union with, the authority of the stronghold!" In other words, he has come into close fellowship with the dominance of lust, pride, arrogance, and disobedience.

He had crossed the line. Turning back was no longer a consideration. Samson was a captive of the grip on his life he had refused to deal with since he initially pursued his Philistine wife.

> **HE HAD CROSSED THE LINE. TURNING BACK WAS NO LONGER A CONSIDERATION.**

As we will see, he was ready to be enticed by *another* Philistine harlot. The stronghold has indeed taken control!

## Not a Casual Matter

Friend, we can reach a place where hardness of heart can paralyze us because of continued disobedience to our Heavenly Father.

When casual, blasé treatment of the sacred things of God becomes commonplace in our lives, a capturing stronghold is not too far behind! That's why we must keep the holy things of God in a sacred place on the mantle of our hearts. I'm not referring to religious statues or pictures, but *holy things* such as being kind and tenderhearted one to another, forgiving, loving and helping each other. These are the attributes which keep our hearts soft and pliable in the hands of the Potter. They also prevent Satan from taking control.

Make no mistake, what we practice on a consistent basis is what develops and dominates our behavior.

*WHAT YOU REHEARSE AND PRACTICE ON A DAILY BASIS BECOMES YOUR INSTINCTIVE BEHAVIOR WHEN PRESSURE IS APPLIED TO YOUR LIFE.*

If you constantly yield to anger, you'll find reasons to lose your temper at anything which doesn't agree or comply with your way of thinking. The opposite is also true. If you practice love, mercy and grace, it will flow from you without you even being aware! Your first reaction to situations will be a desire to demonstrate love and kindness—even when it may not be deserved. This is the type of stronghold we should allow to be preeminent in our lives.

## "Run it Again!"

Let me share a life lesson I learned from my days as a football player.

What you rehearse and practice on a daily basis becomes your instinctive behavior when pressure is applied to your life. Allow me to explain.

In preparation for a game, we would often practice the same play dozens of times. To be honest, it became quite monotonous! Just when you thought you could run this play in your sleep, the coach would say, "Run it again!"

The reason for this is simple. During practice, the pressure on you is minimal. The fans are not in the stands and the game day atmosphere is nonexistent.

**YOUR MIND AND BODY RESPOND TO THE TRAINING, NOT TO THE STRESS OF THE MOMENT.**

In a few days, however, all this will change! The coach knows that by repeating a play over and over again during practice, it will become "second nature" to you.

When the big game arrives and that particular play is called, the intense pressure doesn't affect you. Your mind and body respond to the training, not to the stress of the moment. The fans, the score and the clock all become secondary. You've run this play so often in practice it is now automatic.

With God's help, let us rehearse the "right things" when no one is looking so our reactions will be correct when the pressures of life try to take us out!

## Clear-Headed Decisions

I want to emphasize again the danger of disobeying God's Word. Samson strayed from his Nazarite vow that plainly stated he could have no wine or strong drink. Why did the Lord include this particular command?

I believe God did not want any substance other than His Holy Spirit to influence the decisions a Nazarite made. He wanted the "man of God" to be clear in his thought process so he could hear from heaven concerning his choices.

The truth is, it doesn't take much alcohol to affect our decision making. Today, we don't take a Nazarite vow, but we are called to live exemplary lives of holiness before our God and others.

## A Question of Conduct

I am often asked as a minister how I feel about drinking alcoholic beverages.

While I am aware varied opinions exist, permit me to share my personal encounters with drinking.

*IT TOOK QUITE SOME TIME FOR MY BEHAVIOR TO LINE UP WITH MY BELIEF.*

In 1973, as a student at West Virginia University, I became a born again believer. It was a real experience with God. However, even though my conversion was legitimate, my mind was in need of some serious renewing! In other words, it took quite some time for my behavior to line up with my belief.

Drinking was a big part of my college life. Almost every weekend was spent in either mild, moderate, or extreme

95

drinking situations. My love for Jesus was one hundred percent genuine, yet my affection for Budweiser was real as well!

During this time, I began to develop a reputation on campus. People knew who I was because of football—as well as my vocal proclamations about being a Christian.

When I was interviewed on television because of sports, I would always give the Lord credit for the success I had accomplished. This brought about some unexpected consequences.

## Where's the Separation?

By the time I was a junior, people would see me in bars and say, "Hey, aren't you Al Gluchoski, the ball player? I heard you were a Christian, what are you doing in a place like this?"

Others would ask, "If you are a Christian, why are you drinking that beer?"

*"IF YOU ARE A CHRISTIAN, WHY ARE YOU DRINKING THAT BEER?"*

They believed being a follower of Christ meant you should also be living a separated life, and my drinking did not seem too "separated" to them!

Defensively, I would respond with, "Well, Jesus drank wine." Another response was, "The Bible says to have a little wine for the stomach's sake."

In truth, these were excuses to allow me to fulfill the

lusts of my flesh!

## What's Most Important?

It becomes a question of motive. Why do you crave the beer? Why do you want a "little wine"? To me, if my drinking alcohol is going to weaken my Christian witness, it's just not worth it! It is more important to be a godly example to others.

My flesh and it's desire for wine should not harm my testimony to someone for whom Jesus shed His precious blood!

I fully realize this may seem to be a "legalistic" approach to the matter. I've heard people say, "I was raised in an Italian family and we drank wine at every meal." I've wanted to ask, "Oh, you had wine with your corn flakes at breakfast?"

The truth is, no matter from what family background we hail (mine was a clan of Polish beer drinkers from New Jersey), we are now in a *new* family, the redeemed family of God! We must take on the traits of our Heavenly Father!

Let's be honest. Alcohol does affect our decisions.

## "You Brainless Fool!"

One night after several drinks, a college friend and I hopped into my car and we began to drive back to the dorm—down one of those winding West Virginia roads. As I came upon a wooded area, a large deer was standing right in the middle of the highway.

Most people would think, "Slow down, beep your horn"—anything to cause the deer to run off into the woods.

My alcohol-influenced, football-player brain thought, "That deer looks like a linebacker. Let's ram it and see what happens!"

*"THAT DEER LOOKS LIKE A LINEBACKER. LET'S RAM IT AND SEE WHAT HAPPENS!"*

Today, I write this with a clear, sound mind and realize how stupid that decision was.

I accelerated my car and aimed it right for the buck! At the last instant, the deer jumped out of the way and I clipped him on the backside. The animal was fine; my car was not! As the deer leapt to the side of the road, he stopped and looked back at me as if to say, "You brainless fool, don't you know you could've been killed?"

## Is it a Sin?

I realize this is an extreme example of how strong drink can affect decisions, but the fact of the matter remains, alcohol dulls your senses and influences how you think and the choices you make.

You may never have had the desire to hit a deer—or even a linebacker for that matter—but we all have some type of inclination toward sin. An excess of alcohol will certainly help activate that tendency.

So, is it a sin to drink alcoholic beverages? Well, for me it is. That is *my* conviction.

The apostle Paul writes, *"...for whatsoever is not of faith is sin"* (Romans 14:23). It includes what we eat and drink.

I simply cannot consume alcohol in faith. And I refuse to tell someone it's okay to drink because I don't know how their flesh will respond. However, I understand it is typical for the carnal body to desire more than it actually can tolerate, so the tendency for excess exists in all of us. Why take such a risk?

## Losing Respect

I have a friend who pastors a strong, vibrant church in Southern California. Here's what he shared with me on the issue of alcohol.

He tells his congregation, "If I invited you over to my house for dinner, and you looked in my refrigerator and saw a six pack of beer and maybe a bottle of wine, would you lose respect for me?"

His entire congregation responded, "Yes!"

The reason being, alcohol is associated with more "unholy" things than it is with "holy" things—especially in the United States. The evening news is filled with alcohol-related traffic deaths and violent murders brought on by its abuse. Plus, far too many homes have been destroyed by the behavior of alcoholic husbands and wives.

## *"Beer Glasses!"*

Finally, strong drink also activates a desire for sexual promiscuity. When most men get together to drink, they don't discuss the recent sale held at Nordstrom's last week! Instead, they develop wandering eyes and look at potential female candidates for a sexual encounter.

You may have heard the statement, "She looked good because I was wearing beer glasses." Forgive my crudeness, but that bar room phrase simply means the man settled for an unattractive woman who "looked good to me after I had about twelve beers!"

How sad and demeaning. No, I cannot give my approval to a substance which has such a degrading potential.

However we choose to view this subject, one thing is certain: because Samson allowed strongholds of sin to enter his life and grow, his flesh became out of control!

I know your Heavenly Father has a far better plan for you.

*When you make a deliberate choice to disconnect from God, the anointing will disconnect from you.*

– Al Gluchoski

7

# A "BAD HAIR DAY"

In case you hadn't noticed, Samson was always hanging around the wrong places—with the wrong people.

After his fateful journey to Gaza, the Bible describes how he traveled to the valley of Sorek, a place of the finest Palestine vineyards. There, he *"loved a woman... whose name was Delilah"* (Judges 16:4). Her very name means "to be brought down low!"

Without question, Samson should have exercised more caution and restraint in the places he visited. It's been said, "If you are not supposed to go swimming, then quit hanging around the pool!"

Samson probably thought he was strong enough to handle any situation that crossed his path. Powerful personalities have the tendency to feel the same way about themselves.

## "Blind Love"

*I BELIEVE IT WAS "BLIND LOVE," SINCE THIS LEADER WITH SUCH GREAT POTENTIAL DID NOT SEE BENEATH HER SURFACE.*

Many biblical scholars believe Delilah was a temple prostitute and I agree with them. As we will learn, she certainly was "paid off" to use her sexual wiles to pursue this champion. The Bible says of a harlot: *"For she hast cast down many wounded: yea, many strong men have been slain by her"* (Proverbs 7:26).

In Samson's case, Delilah was the perfect woman for the job!

We don't know how they met, or how long they were together. Scripture only tells us Samson *loved* her. I believe it was "blind love" since this leader with such great potential did not see beneath her surface. He did not discern her true motives and schemes.

## 5,500 Pieces of Silver

The five lords of the Philistines approached Delilah and suggested, *"Entice him, and see wherein his great strength lieth, and by what means we may prevail against him, that we may bind him to afflict him: and we will give thee every one of us eleven hundred pieces of silver"* (Judges 16:5).

What an offer! That's a combined purse of 5,500 pieces of silver just for prying and learning his secret. In her mind, she had just won the Philistine lottery— and all that was required was for her to do what she did best!

> **PERHAPS THIS MIGHTY MAN WAS THINKING, "I'VE WON EVERY ENCOUNTER WITH THE PHILISTINES TO DATE. WHAT POSSIBLE HARM CAN THIS WOMAN CAUSE ME?**

Delilah does as she has been asked and tries to coerce Samson to tell her the source of his great strength.

At that point, Samson should have questioned her motives! Get a clue, Samson!

Perhaps this mighty man was thinking, "I've won every encounter with the Philistines to date. What possible harm can this woman cause me?"

# A Hidden Agenda?

Allow me to pause for a moment and speak directly to church leaders. Be careful to discern the motives of individuals who question you and the decisions you make. Stay alert to the kind of probing inquires used to "innocently" explore your private matters. They are often veiled with a false sense of concern for your well being, yet their objective may be to discover hidden cracks in your armor so they can strike you at your weak point!

A hostile takeover of your authority may be the eventual goal.

Remember, leaders don't need to air their dirty laundry just so others can "better relate" to them. At times this may be tempting, but I look for a leader who will encourage me to strive for spiritual growth.

Certainly I'm aware not all questions have a hidden agenda. It is only common-sense wisdom to be cautious about revealing information to those who may not have your best interest at heart. Unfortunately, this attitude is sometimes present in the church.

> IT IS ONLY COMMON-SENSE WISDOM TO BE CAUTIOUS ABOUT REVEALING INFORMATION TO THOSE WHO MAY NOT HAVE YOUR BEST INTEREST AT HEART.

106

## The Ropes Melted

Not at all worried, Samson tells Delilah to tie him up with seven new moist cords, and he will become weak, like any other man. So she does as he says!

The waiting adversaries were hiding in the chamber when Delilah yelled, "The Philistines be upon thee, Samson" (Judges 16:9).

With one "anointed flex," those cords melted off of him as if burned by fire!

Seeing she had been deceived, Delilah complains, "You've mocked and told me lies. Tell me how you can be bound!"

Samson eggs her on with a second story: "Bind me with new unused ropes, and I'll be like any other man." You guessed it! Delilah ties him with the new ropes, then once again yells: "The Philistines be upon thee!"

**WITH ONE "ANOINTED FLEX" THOSE CORDS MELTED OFF OF HIM AS IF BURNED BY FIRE!**

The scene is repeated as Samson breaks the new ropes, freeing himself as if they were mere strings!

I think we are seeing a pattern. He is toying with her – yet in doing so, Samson is also trifling with God's anointing. Remember, Samson is strong because of a divine touch, not because he works out at the Israeli Health Club!

107

Until now, Samson has used the anointing primarily to destroy Philistines—which was God's purpose for these sudden outbursts of strength. Now, he is abusing his gift to cavort with a harlot.

When you abnormally use something it will be removed from you care. Battered wives will leave husbands; abused children will be taken from the custody of abusive parents; and in the spiritual realm, abused anointings will be removed from those who do not care for them properly.

## Seven Locks

Delilah is far from finished. This deceiving woman is not about to give up until those 5,500 pieces of silver are safe in her bank account!

**"YOU'VE BEEN MOCKING ME, AND LYING AS WELL! TELL ME HOW WE CAN BIND YOU UP!"**

The scripture is not clear concerning the time frame in which Delilah continues to wear down Samson. It was certainly over a period of several days, perhaps even a few weeks. We know, however, this type of treatment had worked on Samson before, with his former Philistine wife. Sadly, it was a lesson he didn't learn.

Delilah tells him, "You've been mocking me, and lying as well! Tell me how we can bind you up."

Samson responds, *"If thou weavest the seven locks of my head with the web"*(Judges 16:13).

That sounded promising. So Delilah lulled Samson into falling asleep, then wove his hair into the web.

## The Web of Deceit

In those days the web was used to weave and make rugs, blankets and clothing. The Bible indicates it was attached to a beam anchored to the wall for support. Samson's long, flowing hair is now woven into this rug-making machine!

After fastening his hair with a pin, she woke him up, again yelling, "The Philistines be upon thee, Samson!"

**THE EVER-PERSISTENT DELILAH STILL WASN'T FINISHED.**

Scripture describes how *"he awaked out of his sleep, and went away with the pin of the beam, and with the web"* (v.14)—and his hair was still attached. That must have been a sight to see!

## "Vexed Unto Death!"

The ever-persistent Delilah still wasn't finished. She beguilingly whispered in his ear, *"How canst thou say, I love thee, when thine heart is not with me? thou hast mocked me these three times, and hast not told me wherein thy great strength lieth"* (v.15).

Samson was weakening. She pressed him daily with her words and urged him to divulge his secret source of physical power. Scripture tells us that as she persisted, *"his soul was vexed unto death"* (v.16).

His will was worn out! Interestingly, the word vexed means, "to cut down," but also is interpreted "to harvest." Samson is about to be trapped and will receive a harvest for the poor stewardship of God's anointing he has demonstrated over and over again.

## What's Different?

Finally, Samson succumbs and tells Delilah the secret no earthly person had ever heard. He confessed, *"There hath not come a razor upon mine head; for I have been a Nazarite unto God from my mother's womb: if I be shaven, then my strength will go from me, and I shall become weak, and be like any other man"* (v.17).

Personally, I don't think Samson ever believed that by revealing to her his secret, he would lose his strength. It was the *only* vow he had not broken, but consider it from his perspective. He likely thought, "I didn't lose my strength when I ate the grapes. I was still strong after drinking the wine. And my power didn't diminish after touching the dead bodies. Why should this time be any different?"

Remember, Samson actually believed his special gift

was the result of his own ability and strength. "God may have given it to me, but it's really mine!"

In a moment we'll see how this is revealed in scripture.

## Time for a Shave!

When Delilah realized Samson had told her everything that was in his heart, she called for the five Philistine lords to come immediately. They arrived, with the money in their hands (v.18).

**THERE, IN SATAN'S BEAUTY SALON, THE HAIRCUT WAS COMPLETE.**

The Bible records: *"...she made him sleep upon her knees; and she called for a man, and she caused him to shave off the seven locks of his head; and she began to afflict him, and his strength went from him"* (v.19).

There, in Satan's Beauty Salon, the haircut was complete and Samson was a transformed man. Delilah began to "afflict" him—to slap and abuse him. His strength had totally vanished.

## It's Gone!

By this time, Delilah was accustomed to touching Samson's body, but now she could tell this wasn't the same man.

Things had dramatically changed. To her, Samson didn't feel the same as he did before the haircut. What was the difference? The anointing had departed, and Delilah could tell this just by touching him. The sad truth is the Philistine harlot knew the anointing was gone, but the man of God did not!

Without question, Samson fully expected to still be anointed after he woke up from his haircut. Notice his first words: *"I will go out as at other times before, and shake myself"* (v.20).

## A Horrible Realization

**HE AWAKENED TO A WORLD HE WAS UNFAMILIAR WITH.**

Once more, Samson thought he was still in control, unaware *"the Lord was departed from him"* (v.20).

He awakened to a world he was unfamiliar with, a world with no power—no divine strength from God. What a horrible realization that must have been.

Samson had no one to blame for this but himself. Delilah was simply a tool of Satan to finish the job Samson had earlier started. The stronghold in his life finally brought him down to that of a normal, average person, far from God's anointing.

Now, he is experiencing the true harvest of being an unwise steward of the anointing which he has "sown" time and time again.

## A Slave

The results were disastrous. The Philistines not only captured Samson, they gouged out his eyes, and placed him in the prison of Gaza (the stronghold) where he was forced to grind at the grist mill of the enemies of God.

**HE SANK FROM BEING AN ANOINTED MAN, TO BECOMING A SLAVE OF GOD'S ENEMIES.**

He sank from being an anointed man, to becoming a slave of God's enemies, working for Dagon (the god of grain) at the Philistine mill. The stronghold had captured him and caused him to lose his purpose and vision. It was definitely a "bad hair day" for Samson!

## The Disconnect

Was it just the action of a razor cutting Samson's locks that caused the loss of such a great anointing? Did God say, "Okay Samson, the haircut is the last straw!"?

I believe it was much more than being shaved because of a harlot. Certainly his hair symbolized what remained of his sacred Nazarite vow to God, and to cut it was an act of disobedience. Consider this: the Bible says Samson told Delilah *"all his heart"* (Judges 16:17) when he revealed his position as a Nazarite.

In being totally transparent, Samson was stating his covenant was no longer sacred to him—in any respect. By pouring out his innermost secrets to her, he emptied himself of any connection to the vow of the Nazarite.

> **THE CHOICES WE MAKE DETERMINE OUR QUALITY OF LIFE AND OUR EVENTUAL DESTINY.**

Samson basically walked away from his call and purpose, telling Delilah, "You mean more to me than God."

Whatever degree of sacred commitment may still have remained in Samson before the haircut, it was released in that moment. By making a deliberate choice to disconnect from God, the anointing also disconnected from him. The haircut "sealed it" as final.

## Stay on Course!

As Christians, it is imperative to understand who we are allowing to influence our decisions. The choices we make determine our quality of life and our eventual destiny. Long ago, King Solomon wrote: *"He that walketh with wise men shall be wise: but a companion of fools shall be destroyed"* (Proverbs 13:20).

Over the years I've seen Christians steer off God's course because they became entrapped by a "Delilah." Some wound up in tragic situations because they allowed the wrong individuals to pressure them into a poor decision.

Charles Spurgeon once said, "There are a thousand razors with which the devil can shave off the locks of a consecrated man without his knowing it."

Remember, we are responsible for the options we choose. Let's surround ourselves with devoted, godly people who can speak faith and wisdom into our lives.

Don't allow a Delilah to schedule your next haircut!

*Never get caught praying the "Let me die with the Philistines" prayer.*

– Al Gluchoski

**8**

# GOD'S NOT FINISHED!

Oh, how the mighty had fallen!

The promised deliverer was no longer sitting on the pedestal as judge of Israel. Now he was bound with brass fetters, grinding grain behind prison walls.

Yet, in that humiliating position, God still wasn't through with Samson—the Lord's mercy endures forever.

Scripture records, *"...the hair of his head began to grow again after he was shaven"* (Judges 16:22). This meant the potential of his power was being renewed.

Please understand, there was nothing magical about Samson's hair. Its growth does, however, represent

119

something significant. If you recall, the Nazarite vow states if the person sins by contact with a dead body, he is to shave his head, go through cleansing, and be given a fresh start as a Nazarite (Numbers 6). The previous days of his separation are considered lost days, but he now has a new beginning!

**GOD GRACED SAMSON WITH A "FRESH START."**

In Samson's case, perhaps grinding at the mill has caused him to rethink his motives and priorities. Has repentance and cleansing occurred? Regardless of how we view this, God graced Samson with a "fresh start." I believe the Lord does this to honor His own Word.

## Blind and Bound!

On a Philistine holy day where Dagon, their god, was being revered, thousands of Philistines, along with the five lords, gathered to thank Dagon for delivering Samson into their hands.

The people sang and rejoiced, *"Our god hath delivered into our hands our enemy, and the destroyer of our country, which slew many of us"* (Judges 16:24).

In this atmosphere of merriment, they led blind and bound Samson out in front of the crowd to mock and make fun of him. There, at the temple, they *"set him between the pillars"* (v. 25).

Then Samson said to the person who held him by the hand, *"Suffer me that I may feel the pillars whereupon the house standeth, that I may lean upon them"* (v.26).

Now, in this final moment of desperation, being made "sport" of by the jeering crowds, Samson cries out to the Almighty, praying, *"O Lord God, remember me, I pray thee, and strengthen me, I pray thee, only this once, O God, that I may be at once avenged of the Philistines for my two eyes"* (v.28).

## Still Bitter

*I DON'T SEE REPENTANCE IN THIS PRAYER— ONLY THE DESIRE FOR REVENGE FOR THE LOSS OF HIS TWO EYES!*

At the risk of sounding too critical of Samson, the only other scripture which records he called on God was when he was dying of thirst!

In my view, I don't see repentance in this prayer—only the desire for revenge for the loss of his two eyes!

Suffering at the grist mill evidently hasn't changed Samson, rather it seems to have placed the stronghold of vengeance back to work in his life!

In my experience as a minister, I've seen many people suffer. Some become better, others grow bitter.

## The Pillars

The temple area was packed with thousands of men, women and children—plus, all the lords of the Philistines were present.

There, in an atmosphere of scorn, *"Samson took hold of the two middle pillars upon which the house stood, and on which it was borne up, of the one with his right hand, and of the other with his left"* (v.29).

As he held those two support pillars, he cried out, *"Let me die with the Philistines"* (v.30).

**IN A FINAL DISPLAY OF GOD'S AWESOME POWER, SAMSON PUSHED DOWN THE PILLARS.**

In a final display of God's awesome power, Samson pushed down the pillars and caused the structure to topple and fall, killing all who were in that place, including Samson.

Many died instantly, others were trampled to death by the stampeding throng.

The Bible declares, *"the dead which he slew at his death were more than they which he slew in his life"* (v.30).

## An Unfinished Task

What a tragic end of a life that never fully completed the tasks God assigned him to accomplish. I suppose it can be said Samson was the wedge that "began" to deliver Israel from Philistine bondage. Yet, I believe his impact could have been far greater—and longer lasting—than the damage he inflicted!

Personally, I will pray the "prayer of faith," the "prayer of petition," and the "prayer of consecration." You won't, however, catch me repeating the "Let me die with the Philistines" prayer! I don't suggest you pray that either!

## *What Could Have Been!*

Allow me to take another view of the story. What would have happened if Samson had prayed like this? "Lord, forgive me for the poor stewardship I showed towards your calling. I repent for being such a lousy Nazarite. Lord, give me back my vision, so I can see all these Philistines that I'm about to destroy for your Glory! And Lord, as I push down these pillars, let every brick crush a Philistine, and let every brick miss my new hairy head!"

*I BELIEVE SAMSON COULD HAVE CALLED ON GOD IN TRUE REPENTANCE AND HIS MERCY WOULD HAVE RESTORED HIM.*

I believe Samson could have called on God in true repentance and His mercy would have restored him—not just with a temporary outburst of strength, but to the leadership of Israel.

He had the opportunity to atone at any time and avoid these consequences. I'm convinced it was condemnation—rather than God's will—which caused Samson to pray the "Let me die with the Philistines" prayer.

## Finish the Race!

In the New Testament, the apostle Paul writes, *"For I am ready to be offered, and the time of my departure is at hand. I have fought a good fight, I have finished my course, I have kept the faith"* (2 Timothy 4:6-7).

**SAMSON'S LACK OF GODLY SELF-CONTROL CAUSED HIM TO PREMATURELY REACH THE FINISH LINE.**

It seems clear Paul was not ready to die until he completed the assignment to which Jesus had called him. Starting a race is much easier than finishing one!

If a runner stays in his lane, he will not be disqualified, and his race will be valid—at the appointed destiny, at the right finish line.

Let me encourage you to stay the course and not allow a lack of discipline to knock you out of the race.

Samson's lack of godly self-control caused him to prematurely reach the finish line—not on the timetable God had purposed for his life.

## Can We Be Trusted?

On these pages I've been mentioning Samson's misguided stewardship of God's anointing.

Let me encourage you to read again the story Jesus tells in Matthew 25 of a man who was a poor steward of money his master had given him to take care of. When it was discovered he misused the funds, it was taken from him and given to the man who produced increase with the money for which he was entrusted.

Samson was given the responsibility for delivering Israel from Philistine bondage. He certainly made several attempts, yet Israel was still in servitude to the Philistines even after Samson's death.

## Two Men—Two Destinies

I believe King David became the "ten-talent man" of Matthew 25 who actually received the anointing (and more) Samson squandered. You see, Samson treated the Spirit of God much too casually.

**SAMSON TREATED THE SPIRIT OF GOD MUCH TOO CASUALLY.**

Like Samson, David killed a lion (and a bear). He destroyed the Philistine champion, Goliath! He was also responsible for the defeat of tens of thousands of Philistines! David's mighty army shared the anointing as well—and one of

125

those men killed 300 foes at one time with only a spear!

Again, like Samson, David displayed moral failures. But there was a distinct difference: David repented, and asked God not to take His Presence or His Spirit from him. He did not want to lose the heavenly anointing, so he treated it with the appropriate respect.

David saw a connection between sin and the eventual loss of God's touch. On the other hand, Samson did not and the results were tragic. After many generations, Israel finally became free from Philistine dominance under the reign of King David—the man after God's own heart.

> AFTER MANY GENERATIONS, ISRAEL FINALLY BECAME FREE FROM PHILISTINE DOMINATION UNDER THE REIGN OF KING DAVID—THE MAN AFTER GOD'S OWN HEART.

## Power to Overcome

Some may think I've been too hard on Samson in what I've shared in this book. It is my strong conviction if Samson were alive today, he would be much harder on himself than I have ever been, and would pen a book to warn people of the consequences of living the kind of life he did!

I salute and honor Samson for the courage and boldness he displayed! After all, I've never faced 1,000 Philistines who wanted to skin me alive! However, I have encountered other temptations Samson faced—and have found through Jesus Christ we can overcome every adversity that tries to separate us from the path the Lord has planned.

Thank God for His amazing mercy, grace and power. It keeps us strong!

*If we humble ourselves, God will do the exalting. If we exalt ourselves, we will be humbled.*

– Al Gluchoski

# 9

# WHAT DOES IT MEAN TO ME?

O h, what life-changing lessons we can learn from observing the life of Samson.

While it is true we have a "better covenant with better promises" than Samson had, the New Testament writers exhort us to live our lives "holy and acceptable unto God."

One of Samson's glaring mistakes was not walking with a healthy fear of God. If he had, he would have dealt with temptation with more wisdom, and perhaps avoided sin.

Scripture tells us, *"...by the fear of the Lord men depart from evil"* (Proverbs 16:6) and *"The fear of the*

*Lord is the beginning of wisdom"* (Proverbs 9:10). Even more, *"...the fear of the Lord prolongeth days"*(Proverbs 10:27) Samson's life ended far too soon!

Today, we are not asked to take a Nazarite vow since we are holy and separated by virtue of the blood of Jesus. As a result, our actions should display the inward working of the sacrifice Christ made.

**OUR ACTIONS SHOULD DISPLAY THE INWARD WORKING OF THE SACRIFICE CHRIST MADE.**

God has honored us with the privilege of walking free from sin. We can *all* make the proper choices in response to temptation, and not submit to Satan's dominance.

I'm not saying we will never stray, but as we grow closer to the Father, sin's attraction will diminish and it's hold on us will be destroyed! Your "want to" will change.

## "Is it Okay?"

In my early days as a Christian at West Virginia University, I had many of the same tendencies regarding sin that Samson possessed.

A good friend, who was part of a campus ministry, would meet with me weekly to share Bible study and answer any concerns I had about the Christian walk. Most of my questions were, "Is it okay to do this?" "Is it okay to do that?"

The truth is, I was wanting to see how close I could come to the edge of sin and not fall in! I was wondering, "What can I get away with and still be okay with God?"

These are the child-like first steps experienced by many young believers.

When Samson explored the vineyards of Timnath as a young man, I doubt he went there with the intention to sin. His curiosity about wine and grapes may have innocently led him astray. However, iniquity was the ultimate result of this innocent journey. We are to avoid even the *appearance* of sin.

*I WAS WONDERING, "WHAT CAN I GET AWAY WITH AND STILL BE OKAY WITH GOD?"*

## Escape the Snare

The Word tells us to stay away from the things that can potentially knock us off the course God has planned for our future. Jesus says, *"If thy right hand offend thee, cut it off"* (Matthew 5:30).

When an animal is caught in a trap, it will act violently trying to get out! I have even seen cases where animals have chewed off their own leg or paw rather than remain there and get skinned!

If you need to take extreme measures to avoid the entrapment Satan has set for your life, do it! No, don't literally cut off your hand, but take the necessary steps to escape the snare and be set free from sin's effect.

## A Warning

I am convinced the vast majority of today's Christian leaders are sincere and godly people with a desire to please the Lord. I also believe these same individuals can be trusted with the stewardship of the gifting and callings God has bestowed upon them. Yes, some may miss the mark and perhaps sin, but they turn quickly to Christ with repentant hearts and a desire to make things right—determined not to cause further offense towards God or man.

**OLD TESTAMENT EXAMPLES "ARE WRITTEN FOR OUR ADMONITION."**
*– 1 CORINTHIANS 10:11*

I have, however, also seen how the same attitude which overtook Samson has begun to work in the lives of some precious Christian men and women. According to Paul, the Old Testament examples *"are written for our admonition* (1Corinthians 10:11). They are a warning not to follow the same pattern of behavior that caused early saints to stumble and fall.

## The Road of Humility

We are to always give God the credit for whatever good is accomplished in and through our lives—being aware we are just the vessel through which God has chosen to work and bring blessing to others.

Follow the advice of the apostle Peter: *"Humble yourselves therefore under the mighty hand of God, that he may exalt you in due time"* (1 Peter 5:6). Let's make sure we don't get that order reversed! If we humble ourselves, God will do the exalting. If we exalt ourselves, we will be humbled. Ask Samson!

The Word tells us: *"A man's pride shall bring him low: but honor shall uphold the humble in spirit"* (Proverbs 29:23).

A man of humility is not a weak person, but one who places himself in total submission to God and His Word—aware of the Lord's desires and willing to obey His directions. He's not pushing his own agenda.

**IF WE EXALT OURSELVES, WE WILL BE HUMBLED. ASK SAMSON!**

The original meaning of the word humble was "harnessed power"—and it certainly doesn't indicate weakness. The term described a person of focused strength, with God as the controller! Such a man is headed for promotion in the Kingdom.

We need God *gracing* us, not *resisting* us!

One of the more damaging effects of pride is presented by King Solomon when he warns: *"Pride goeth before destruction, and a haughty spirit before a fall"* (Proverbs 16:18)

This scripture certainly describes what happened to Samson, but it also reveals what will become our fate if we allow haughtiness to take root in our lives!

**GOD'S PLAN FOR US IS FOR GOOD AND NOT EVIL!**

God's plan for us is for good and not evil! Pride will detour that destiny and place us on a road where the ultimate end is destruction.

## Two Traps

Let's keep our motives pure—both where finances and members of the opposite sex are concerned. Do not be seduced by either.

Handle money with godly care so you will not be entangled by it's allure. Realize it is not evil; rather, it is a means to help you accomplish God's calling. Only when money becomes the prime motivator of our actions does trouble begin.

Those who lust after and covet wealth, *"have erred from the faith, and pierced themselves through with many sorrows"* (1 Timothy 6:10).

Sure, we all need money to exist—some more than others. It's how we handle it that matters. Jesus says, *"...if we have not been faithful in the unrighteous mammon* (money), *who will commit to your trust the true riches?"* (Luke 16:11).

## The Money Motive

I believe how we treat money in relation to God's Kingdom determines the degree of spiritual insights and operations (true riches) that God can entrust to our care.

Money can also be a *positive* motivator if used in the proper context. For example, young David asked what the reward would be to the man who killed Goliath. He was told, *"..the king will enrich him with great riches, and will give him his daughter, and make his father's house free in Israel"* (1 Samuel 17:25).

**MONEY CAN BE A POSITIVE MOTIVATOR IF USED IN THE PROPER CONTEXT.**

Two out of the three rewards involved money! In this case, it served as a motive for David to produce a godly result! Having riches is not wrong or sinful. We must, however, respect our finances and its God-ordained purpose for our lives.

## Your Thought Life

The second danger is the temptation of the opposite sex—a major factor in Samson's demise!

If you are a married person, you have no business even thinking about another man or woman. In reality, it is in the *thought* life where adultery or fornication

137

begins. Such thoughts cannot be entertained!

At the writing of this book, I've been in full time ministry for more than 16 years. Without exception, each year I have either been told of or had to counsel someone who fell morally because they failed to "cast down" imaginations when the wrong thoughts entered their minds. Some have been ministers, others Christians who gave in to their earthly desires.

**TRAGEDIES COULD HAVE BEEN AVOIDED IF THE MIND HAD BEEN CONTROLLED.**

In all cases, the problem began in their thought process—and that's where it should have ended! Many of the marriages survived the pain, while others did not! Tragedies could have been avoided if the mind had been controlled.

## No Excuses!

When dealing with the issue, I've often heard this response from those who fall into the sin of adultery: "My wife doesn't appreciate me. I have needs too, you know!" Or, "My husband does not understand or pay attention to me. He does not meet my emotional needs!"

There are a myriad of excuses which can be voiced, yet none of them are valid. There is *no excuse* for the sin of adultery!

Sure, the needs of husbands and wives are real. Yet,

even though such desires are being neglected by either party, it's still no reason to break your vow!

When God said, "Thou shalt not commit adultery," He knew the situations married couples would be facing. He still said, "Don't do it!"

## Your Way of Escape

The act of adultery is a demonstration of selfishness! Scripture clearly states: *"But whoso committeth adultery with a woman lacketh understanding"* (Proverbs 6:32).

We can paraphrase the verse and say, "Committing adultery is stupid!" The straying spouse is one who has no strength of character.

God is more than able to help and guide you through all the misunderstandings, rejection and whatever emotional stress has resulted in the temptation of adultery.

**THE ACT OF ADULTERY IS A DEMONSTRATION OF SELFISHNESS.**

Remember this: God tells us He won't allow you to be tempted in an area you can't handle! (1 Corinthians 10:13). It may not be easy, but the Lord says He will provide you with a way of escape!

Sometimes it seems our problems are just too overwhelming. Be encouraged. God's Word gives us the answer to every situation we will ever face. His grace is always available in our time of need.

# A High Cost!

We must see the connection between continued sin and the loss of fulfilled purpose. King David recognized this fact. So did Joseph when tempted by Potipher's wife. He knew this "great wickedness" would cost him the loss of his dream and destiny.

Please realize there is a high price for sin if we don't police ourselves and change. Our purpose is important. The touch of God's Spirit is too valuable to lose!

*THE TOUCH OF GOD'S SPIRIT IS TOO VALUABLE TO LOSE!*

We must not sacrifice the Spirit's anointing on the altar of pride, lust and other areas. Your life and the lives of others are depending on your stewardship of that precious gifting. With God's help, you are more than able to accomplish the job and be exactly what God has called you to be!

In studying Samson's life, I don't think anyone can be neutral in their feelings toward him. I personally experienced a wide range of emotions while writing these words.

As we look at his heroics or his failures, I believe we can all find a little bit of ourselves in Samson. As we do, let's make the needed changes.

When I reach heaven, next to Jesus, one of the first men I want to meet is Samson! I look forward to shaking his hand and thanking him for being used by God in such an awesome anointing, and just in case he is reading this book, I hope he forgets where he threw that jawbone!

## Your Ark of Safety

The church is not perfect and has its "Samsons" along with other problems. It seems practically every denomination and church group have endured scandals which have been amplified to the secular world. Satan uses such diversions to keep people away from the house of God and hinders their growing relationship with the Lord Jesus Christ.

Remember Noah's ark? I'm sure the odor of those animals was not always the most pleasant aroma, yet the ark was still the safest place to be!

The church may have it's problems, it may even "smell" at times, but it has always been and always will be the safest place to abide!

I pray God will anoint you and bless your life as you learn from His Word and become a strong, vibrant, living testimony to the grace of our Lord and Savior, Jesus Christ.

For a Complete list of Ministry Products or to Schedule the Author for Speaking Engagements, Contact:

Al Gluchoski Ministries
P.O. Box 821818
Ft. Worth, TX 76182

Phone: 817-431-6146
Fax: 817-431-3503
Internet: www.algministries.org